But.....
did you see
the roses?

Written by
Judi Bean

To order additional copies of this book, contact:
Xlibris
1-888-795-4274
www.Xlibris.com
Orders@Xlibris.com

Introduction

I welcome you to my book of poetry. This is for the grandmothers all over the world who have the opportunity to grasp hold of the children entrusted to you in individual capacities. Open your heart for them to surprise you. At the risk of using an all too familiar cliché', "Life is short". I implore you to jump in and enjoy the ride with the time you have.

Dedication

This book is dedicated to my sister, Debby, who inspired me.
God blessed her with an incomparable sense of humor.

Jason and Meggin

My First Born

On November 29 of '72
Went to the hospital. A baby was due.

The air was balmy, a little like May.
Not as the weather we'd see the next day!

The doctor would scurry; he needed to go
See a football game, the 'bedlam", you know!

I labored all day and into the night.
Something was wrong. This just wasn't right.

The family was there and cheered me on.
But still yet, the hours were long.

My husband, my mama there with me throughout.
I wasn't very pleasant. Sometimes I would shout!

Then at two the next morning with snow on the tree
My baby was born, a leader to be.

But not for himself, but to honor the One
Who gave him new life through Jesus, His Son!

Cori and Scott

A little girl in mid-December

A little girl in mid-December.
An easy day, I seem to remember.

Name her Cori, I heard Him proclaim.
A refuge for many, a witness, a flame.

Half of her heart, the other part laughter.
Keep up with her muse? You'll have to be faster!

To her Daddy, she's perfect.
Can do no ill will.

But I know better.
Sometimes she's a pill!

Her husband's her rock, her fortress, her shield.
If they share any traits, it's pretty concealed!

Three "Grand" children – she gave to me.
She's my "baby girl" And always will be.

Kenzie
"The Little Princess (from) The Land o' Plenty"

Morgan

A Surprise Package

Morgan Elizabeth, what can I say......
The world wasn't ready for you that day!

Your dad pushed your mom down that
Hospital hall…..
Hoping you all wouldn't stumble and fall.

Came into this life with a smile on your face….
Who can keep up with your wit and your grace?

Jesus you met as a child really young.
Always let Him control
That sweet little tongue!

Addyson

Shelby

Snow Angels

'Twas a snowy day in December,
The sixth, I seem to remember.
My "Addyson Lee"
Made granddaughter three
Of which she is the fifth member!

Then spring time arrived with a rage.
Another little girl, "Shelby Paige"!
And what do you know…..
In March it did snow.
The world was again a white stage.

God sent down His love,
But not on a dove.
'Twas on angels that year,

Snow Angels so dear.

Nana 11/30/2006

(I wrote this on my last day of work before retirement)

Jack

My Lawyer

Jack Sawyer, Jack Sawyer,
Will you be a lawyer?

Rise to the heights of your mother and father?
A doctor, a preacher,
A farmer, a teacher?

No matter, no worries.
Whatever you be,

Let Jesus guide you.
In Him, you'll be free!

Josh

Funny Face

Josh is the one with curls on his knob.
He's cuddly and loving yet "rough as a cob."

He wrestles with brother and laughs at a fart!
Plunders his sister's crayons and art.

The youngest of three, yet stout as a tree.

He's Papa's hay-hauler……
It's destined to be!

Cole

Cowboy Cole

Cole Bean, Cole Bean,
Did you know that you are
The only one with a "battle scar?"

So fast, so wiry and agile.
But not in the least bit fragile!

You're a Daddy's boy, but even so,

Keeping up with your sisters,
Will sure give you blisters;

And may be a "hard road to hoe"!

The Silver Ball.

The Silver Ball

(A Sonnet)
co-written by Judi Bean and Kenzie Bean

The boys were pumped, as fans were there to cheer.

The 'other' team had all the marks to fear.

Black and Gold were the colors on display.

A trophy stood for us to win that day.

The balls went high and shots and goals were made.

A clock ran down. The lead began to fade.

As refs called "Foul", it seemed unjustified.

The crowd went wild; unleashed and loud, they cried,

"Bad call", "Unfair", they said; and took to feet.

But, nonetheless, touché, the boys were beat.

Sad day for all the fans that made the noise;

But most of all, for coaches and the boys.

Our hearts cry out, as you have made us proud.

Sincerely yours, "The faithful Panther Crowd'.

A Girl Named Gail

(A Sonnet)
written by Morgan Bean

This is a story of a girl named Gail;

How she overcame her life without sight.

Gail woke up once seeing nothing but night.

She was scared because she had to read Braille.

At the beginning all she did was fail.

It was hopeless. Gail became filled with fright.

To seek professional help, she took flight.

She met with doctors from the college, Yale.

The diagnosis showed that she was blind.

A few weeks in Yale, Gail met a blind boy.

He was drawn to her like a turtledove.

He understood her and was very kind.

He taught her to be happy and have joy.

It was not long until they fell in love.

The Gold Ball.

The Gold Ball

Aka "G-L-O-R-I-A"

With honor and grace and talent 'to boot',
The boys took 'the high road', not a short route.

Many long hours and time on their knees
Took them to heights they dared not conceive.

Black and gold jerseys and 'sonic' commotion
Gave life to a crowd as big as the ocean.

Five starters together with more in tow
Played for the victory they soon would know.

A lone free throw in a double would land
A win for a team we think pretty grand!

A Store.

Ode to a Store

(A Sonnet)

The land was purchased and 'talk' went around.

Excitement was stirred. A store for this town?

Dozers, and backhoes, and ditch witches came

Watching and waiting for progress's aim.

Gas tanks were laid and put into place.

Unknown to us, it would be a test case!

But, oh for a year, we relished her picks.

The place to go for a quick dinner's fix.

Pajamas, no make-up, and hair in array,

Semblance of home, "How are you today?"

Then national news came as a sharp bite.

Nothing the little town did could make right.

Sign on the door read, "Closed" one year later.

Back to the web, 'find your store locator.'

Printed in the United States
By Bookmasters